PUFFIN BOOKS

It Takes One to Know One

Gervase Phinn is a teacher, freelance lecturer, author, poet, educational consultant, school inspector, visiting professor of education and, last but by no means least, father of four. Most of his time is spent in schools with teachers and children.

His first book, *The Other Side of the Dale*, was published in March 1998, followed in 2000 by *Over Hill and Dale*. This is his first book for children.

Other books by Gervase Phinn

THE OTHER SIDE OF THE DALE
OVER HILL AND DALE

Gervase Phinn

It Takes One
to Know One

Illustrated by Chris Mould

PUFFIN BOOKS

PUFFIN BOOKS

Published by the Penguin Group
Penguin Books Ltd, 80 Strand, London WC2R 0RL, England
Penguin Putnam Inc., 375 Hudson Street, New York, New York 10014, USA
Penguin Books Australia Ltd, Ringwood, Victoria, Australia
Penguin Books Canada Ltd, 10 Alcorn Avenue, Toronto, Ontario, Canada M4V 3B2
Penguin Books India (P) Ltd, 11 Community Centre, Panchsheel Park, New Delhi – 110 017, India
Penguin Books (NZ) Ltd, Cnr Rosedale and Airborne Roads, Albany, Auckland, New Zealand
Penguin Books (South Africa) (Pty) Ltd, 24 Sturdee Avenue, Rosebank 2196 South Africa

Penguin Books Ltd, Registered Offices: 80 Strand, London WC2R 0RL, England

www.penguin.com

'Classroom Creatures', 'School Trip', 'Book week', 'Class Discussion', 'The Little Chatterbox', 'Bible
Class', 'My Teacher', 'Christmas Presents for Miss', 'Parents' Evening', 'Interrogation in the Nursery',
'Poetry Lesson', 'Farmgirl', 'Asking Questions', 'Mr Lee Teaches Poetry' and 'Once Upon a Time' first
published in Classroom Creatures, by Roselea Publications, 1996
'It Takes One to Know One', edited by John Foster, first published in Crack Another Yolk, by Oxford
University Press, 1996

This collection published 2001
3

Text copyright © Gervase Phinn, 2001
Illustrations copyright © Chris Mould, 2001
All rights reserved

The moral right of the author and illustrator has been asserted

Set in 12/16 Joanna

Made and printed in England by Clays Ltd, St Ives plc

British Library Cataloguing in Publication Data
A CIP catalogue record for this book is available from the British Library

ISBN 0–141–30901–6

Contents

Treasure

Opening the covers of a book
Is like lifting the lid of a treasure chest.
Look inside and you will find
Golden stories and glittering characters.

Some are given a map to show where X marks the spot.
Some are given the precious key to open the lock.
Some are helped to lift the heavy lid.
But for some it will remain hidden treasure.

Father Said

My father said, 'There is no such word as can't!'
Well, I looked it up in the dictionary and there is,
And I told him so.
He got angry.

He can't take a joke my father!

Mother to Son

Eat your breakfast – you should always start the day on
   a full stomach!
Remember to clean your teeth – a bright smile makes all
   the difference!
Wash behind your ears – I can see a tide mark
   from here!
Change that shirt – the collar looks grubby!
Brush your shoes – they're all scuffed!
Change your socks – you can't go to school in those!
Take a clean handkerchief – and give your nose
   a blow!
Straighten that tie – it's at half mast!
Comb your hair – you look like a scarecrow!
Take a jacket – in case it rains!
Put your sandwiches in your bag – you'd lose your head if
   it wasn't screwed on!
Don't forget your school books and I hope you've finished
   all your work!
Be in before it gets dark!

**You'd think at forty-four and a headmaster,
you would be able to make a few decisions for yourself!**

I Only Asked

On Sunday Dominic asked his dad:
'Which is the brightest star?'
'Ask your mum,' his dad replied,
'I have to clean the car.'

On Monday Dominic asked his mum:
'What's a carburettor?'
'Ask your dad,' his mum replied,
'I've got to post this letter.'

On Tuesday Dominic asked his dad,
'What's a UFO?'
'Ask your mum,' his dad replied,
'The grass, it needs a mow.'

On Thursday Dominic asked his dad:
'How tall are kangaroos?'
'Ask your mum,' his dad replied,
'I'm listening to the news.'

On Friday Dominic asked his dad:
'Do all kings have a crown?'
'Ask your mum,' his dad replied,
'I'm going into town.'

On Saturday Dominic asked them both:
'Do you mind me asking things,
About stars and cars and life on Mars
And kangaroos and kings?'

'Of course we don't,' his dad replied,
'Ask questions as you grow.'
'By asking things,' his mother cried,
'That's how you get to know.'
Little Dominic scratched his head,
And simply answered, **'Oh!'**

It Takes One
to Know One

LIBRARIANS take it as read
HISTORIANS take you aback
CARPENTERS take the edge off
REBELS take up cudgels
HOROLOGISTS take one's time
CARDIOLOGISTS take heart
TAXI DRIVERS take you for a ride
SNOOKER PLAYERS take one's cue
KLEPTOMANIACS take it from there
PILOTS take off
PATIENTS take their medicine
HURDLERS take a running jump
COSMETICIANS take a powder
SURGEONS take it out of you
SOLDIERS take steps
DUELLISTS take the point
PURSUERS take after me
HYPOCRITES take on the appearance of
GOOD SAMARITANS take somebody in
LEVITATORS take somebody up on something
WASHERWOMEN take down a peg or two
FOOTBALL MANAGERS take somebody on one side
EXECUTIONERS take something to one's head
BUT ME … I can take it or leave it!

Our Dog Tiny

Mum and Dad said one day:

> Would you like a puppy dog?
> We could get one from the RSPCA.

I said:

> I'd like a big dog, a barking dog,
> A bouncy black and white dog.

Mum said:

> I'd like a floppy dog, a friendly dog,
> A fluffy sit-on-your-knee dog.

Dad said:

> I'd like a mean dog, a lean dog,
> A growling, catch-a-thief dog.

Elizabeth said:

> I don't mind, whatever kind,
> Will be all right for me.

At the pound, we found
Lots and lots of dogs around.

I said:

> I'd like a big dog, a barking dog,
> A bouncy black and white dog.

The keeper said:

> We've got fun dogs, gun dogs,
> Scotty dogs, spotty dogs,
> Snoopy dogs, droopy dogs,

Leaping dogs, sleeping dogs,
Hairy dogs, scary dogs,
Even acrobatic dogs!

Mum said:

I'd like a floppy dog, a friendly dog,
A fluffy sit-on-your-knee dog.

The keeper said:

We've got fat dogs, flat dogs,
Shaggy dogs, scraggy dogs
Small dogs, tall dogs,
Tubby dogs, chubby dogs,
Skinny dogs, mini dogs,
Even currant pudding dogs.

Dad said:

I'd like a mean dog, a lean dog,
A growling, catch-a-thief dog.

The keeper said:

We've got loud dogs, proud dogs,
Rough dogs, tough dogs,
Happy dogs, snappy dogs,
Mad dogs, bad dogs,
Collie dogs, jolly dogs,
'Even multi-coloured dogs.

Elizabeth said:

I don't care whatever's there
Will be just fine for me.

We walked and walked
Around the pound
And peered in every cage we found,
Until at last we all agreed
Upon a mongrel dog, a rag-mop dog
A little bag of bones dog.

We named it Tiny and we took it home.
Since then it's grown and grown.

Dad says: It chews the bumper on my car,
And rests its head on the
breakfast bar.

Mum says: Its growl is like an express train,
The noise will drive me quite
insane.

I say: With giant tusks and iron jaw
It's crunched and munched my
bedroom door.

I don't care, **said little Liz,**
I like him just the way he is.
His tail is white, his paws are black,
Red bristles sprout along his back.
His eyes are of the palest green,
With the longest lashes ever seen.
One ear sticks up, the other down,
One ear is grey, one ear is brown.
I really think it is a shame
That lots of dogs all look the same.
Ours is as different as can be,
And Tiny is the dog for me!

Maths Homework

One, two,
This just won't do!

Three, four,
I've told you before!

Five, six,
Excuses and tricks!

Seven, eight, nine,
Never on time!

Nine, ten,
Not even a pen!

One, two,
I'm tired of you!

Three, four,
Can't take any more!

Five, six, seven,
Why in high heaven

Eight, nine, ten,
Do you forget your
homework,

Again and again and
again and again?

11

Last Request

Major Alexander Phinn
An ancestor of mine,
Was captured by the enemy
Across the River Rhine.
The captain of the firing squad
Asked, 'Is there a last request?'
My Uncle Alex smiled and said,
'Yes please – a bulletproof vest!'

Asking Questions

When I ask my mum, 'What's for tea?'
She smiles and says, 'Wait and see!'

When I ask my dad what things he's done,
He smiles and says, 'In a minute, son.'

When I ask my gran if I can watch TV
'I'll think about it,' she says to me.

When I ask my gramps about the good old days,
'Now you're asking,' he smiles and says.

If I answer the questions my teacher asks me
With 'In a minute' or 'Wait and see,'

I know just what the result would be!

The Little Chatterbox

'Gemma,' said the teacher, 'you've been talking all
    the day.
Natter, natter, natter – you have such a lot to say.
Your little mouth is moving every time I look your way.
I think your mummy has a chatterbox at home.'

'Oh no,' replied the infant, 'we don't have one of those,
With their little furry faces and their funny little toes.
My brother he has asthma and the hairs get up his nose,
So we don't have any animals at home!'

Farmgirl

When she's collected the eggs

And milked the cows,

Groomed the mare

And fed the sows,

Filled the troughs

And stacked the logs,

Cooped the hens

And penned the dogs ...

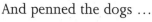

She then begins her homework.

Book Week

'You all come dressed as characters,'
Miss Wilks, our teacher said,
'From all the famous stories
And poems that you've read.
And on Monday in assembly
Everyone will look
And try to guess the character
And recognize the book.'

I went as the Pied Piper
With coat of gold and red
And breeches of bright yellow
And a cap upon my head.
It was made of thick crepe paper
With cardboard belt in brown
But as I walked to school that day
The rain came falling down.

The paper went all soggy
And all the yellow dye
Trickled down my forehead
And I began to cry.
At school I looked a sorry sight
All brown and yellow and sad,
But Miss Wilks, my teacher, dried my eyes
And said, 'It's not that bad.'

The assembly was fantastic,
Everyone was there:
Pinocchio and Captain Hook,
Noddy and Paddington Bear,
Cinderella and Peter Pan,
There was Alice and Mister Toad.
Then Miss Wilks pointed straight at me,
'Oh, and here is The Yellow Brick Road.'

Classroom Creatures

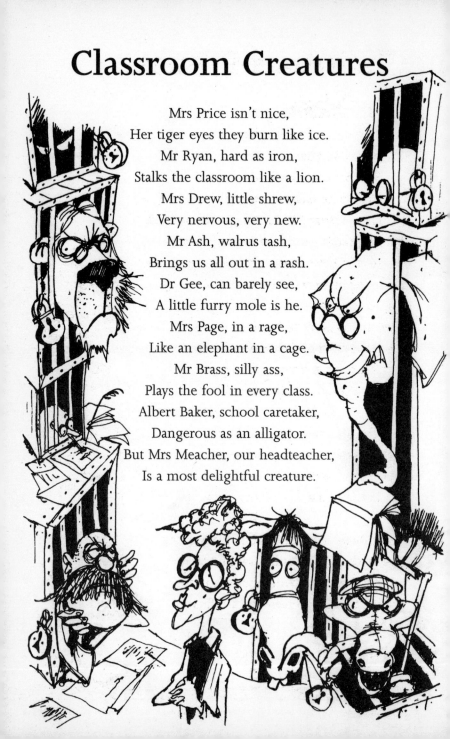

Mrs Price isn't nice,
Her tiger eyes they burn like ice.
Mr Ryan, hard as iron,
Stalks the classroom like a lion.
Mrs Drew, little shrew,
Very nervous, very new.
Mr Ash, walrus tash,
Brings us all out in a rash.
Dr Gee, can barely see,
A little furry mole is he.
Mrs Page, in a rage,
Like an elephant in a cage.
Mr Brass, silly ass,
Plays the fool in every class.
Albert Baker, school caretaker,
Dangerous as an alligator.
But Mrs Meacher, our headteacher,
Is a most delightful creature.

Christmas Presents for Miss

Chocolates in a fancy box –
    For the teacher who is tops!
A tea towel and an oven glove –
    From Gemma Thompson with my love.
A bottle stands in thick brown paper –
    All the best – from Darren Baker.
Perfumed soap from Lee and Chris,
    You're our favourite teacher, Miss.
Flowers in a coloured pot –
    Happy Christmas, Helen Bott.
A china dog with painted face –
    For the teacher who is ace!

And from the nuisance of the class
The Nativity encased in glass.
    I know this year I've been a pain,
    I'm sorry, Miss – with love from Wayne.

And though she's taught for many years,
The teacher's eyes still fill with tears,
For children know the ones who care
And that is why those gifts are there.

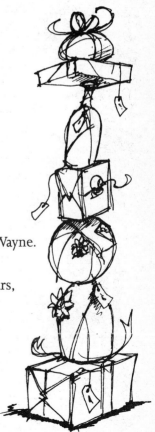

Class Discussion

'In the class discussion, **Jane**, you hardly said a word.
We all aired our opinions but from you we rarely heard.
You sat and stared in silence surrounded by the chatter,
Now tell me, **Jane**, and please be plain,
Is there anything the matter?'

Jane looked up and then she spoke,
Her voice was clear and low:
**'There are many people in this world
Who are rather quiet, you know!'**

Parents' Evening

So you are Matthew's mother
Then you must be his dad?
I'm so very pleased to meet you,
I am extremely glad.
He's such a gifted pupil,
And such a little dear,
There's been a vast improvement
In all his work this year.
His writing is exceptional,
So beautifully neat,
His spelling quite incredible,
His poetry a treat.
His number work is flawless
And his painting so inspired.
He's interested and lively,
And he's never ever tired.
He's amazingly athletic,
And excels in every sport.
Your Matty is the brightest child
That I have ever taught.
I should say he's gifted – he comes top in every test.
In fact in every single subject
Your Matthew is the best!
I must say, Mr and Mrs Flynn,
You're fortunate to have a child like him.

Pardon?

Oh! You're not Matthew Flynn's father,

Then you can't be his mum.

You say I've got the names mixed up.

Oh dear! What have I done?

Well, I'm very, very sorry.

So your child's Matthew Brown.

Well, before I tell you about your son

You had better both sit down!

22

Mr Lee Teaches Poetry

Our English teacher, Mr Lee,
Is very keen on poetry
And every morning he will say:
'We're going to write a poem today.
But please don't waste a lot of time,
In trying to make your poetry rhyme.
In writing there is nothing worse
Than striving desperately in verse
To fit the words into the line,
Just to get a silly rhyme.
So remember in your poem today,
It doesn't have to rhyme – you know!'

Poetry Lesson

'I like your poem, Mandy … but
There are parts which don't sound right.
You say that **stars like diamond chips**
Illuminate the night,
And that **the cold and distant moon**
Gives off an eerie light …
I think that there are better words to use.

'I like your poem, Mandy … but
Be careful with the rhymes.
You say that **from the lonely church**
Came strange and distant chimes,
Reminding you **of far-off days**
And of much happier times …
I think that there are better words to use.

I like your poem, Mandy … but
The images aren't too good.
Instead of **spooky forest glade,**
Insert **the ghostly wood**
And avoid those dreadful gory bits
Especially the blood.
I think that there are better words to use.

'And tell me,' said the teacher,
'Have you anything to say?'
And Mandy said, 'I'd like to ask,

Whose poem is it … anyway?'

Bible Class

Reverend Bright, our vicar,
Came in our class today.
He started with a little talk,
Then we closed our eyes to pray.
He talked about the Bible,
And the prophet Abraham,
How God created everything
And how the world began.
Then he asked us all some questions
About the prophets and the kings,
David and Goliath,
And lots of other things.
'In a very famous garden
Grew an apple on a tree,
And who ate the forbidden fruit?'
And a voice said,

'Wasn't me!'

My Teacher

I'm glad that I'm a pupil
Of Mrs Eddleston,
For every day is wonderful,
Ooh, we do have lots of fun.
There's wooden bricks and building blocks
And sand piled on a tray,
A Wendy House and crates of toys,
To play with all the day.
In the morning when I wave goodbye
To Mummy at the gates,
I see Mrs Eddleston,
Smiling as she waits.
Then I run across the playground
Through a sea of smiling faces
And change into my indoor shoes
(I can do up all my laces!)

I hang my outdoor coat up
On a row of little hooks,
And rush to the Reading Corner
Where there's lots of picture books.
Then Mrs Eddleston starts reading
About the Mermaid and the Whale,
About giants, elves and monsters mean
Or our favourite fairy tale.

And if the story frightens me
I climb up on her knee
And she tells me not to worry
Because it all ends happily.
But I'm sad and very sorry
For I must leave Mrs Eddleston
For now I am a big boy
And I must be moving on.
And though I've shed so many tears,
Enough to fill a pool,
Next year I join the sixth form
At the comprehensive school.

Once Upon a Time

Once upon a time, children, long, long ago,
There lived a …

Big, ugly monster, Miss?

No, David, not a big, ugly monster – a beautiful princess
called Imelda. She had eyes as bright and as green as
sparkling emeralds. She had hair which fell down her back
like a golden waterfall. Her skin was as white …

As a ghost's, Miss?

No, not a ghost's, David. As white as the snow which
covered the fields. Her lips were as red as …

Blood, Miss?

No, not blood, David, as red as cherries. But Princess
Imelda was lonely. How she longed for someone with
whom to play. As the seasons passed she stared out from
the high window of her castle. Then one day something
happened.

Did she fall out, Miss?

No, she didn't fall out, David. She saw in the distance a great cloud of smoke.

A fire-breathing dragon come to eat her up?

David, will you listen! It wasn't a dragon. It was a prince on a great white horse. As he rode over the little bridge …

Did he fall off?

No!

Miss, was there a wicked troll under the bridge?

David! Would you be quiet. There are other children in the class, you know, who might want to say something or ask a question. Now give somebody else a chance. Yes, Amy, have you got a question to ask me?

Yes, Miss.

What is it, dear?

May I go to the toilet please?

School Trip

On our school trip to Scarborough
We got to school on time,
But the coach was caught in traffic
And arrived at half past nine.
Miss Phipps, our teacher, was so cross,
Left standing in the rain
And when the coach pulled up at last
She didn't half complain.
The driver started shouting,
He said there'd been a queue,
But Miss Phipps she said, 'That's no excuse!'
And started shouting too.

On our school trip to Scarborough
The sky turned cold and grey,
Freezing winds blew down the beach
And it rained and rained all day.
Then Sharon slipped on a slimy rock,
And Gordon grazed his knee,
And Colin fell off the castle wall,
And John jumped in the sea.
Then our teacher started shouting
And her voice was loud and high,
And soon we were surrounded
By a crowd of passers-by.

On our school trip to Scarborough
There was really quite a do
When Hazel's hat blew out to sea
And Simon lost a shoe,
And David dropped his flask of soup
Which rolled right off the pier
And landed on the coastguard
Who happened to be near.
Then the coastguard started shouting
When it hit him with a **thwack**
And when David said, 'I'm sorry, mate,
Could you pass my thermos back?'

On our school trip to Scarborough
We all ate tons and tons
Of sticky rock and sandwiches
And jellied eels and buns.
And when the coach left Scarborough
Sam was sick on Chris
And Chris was sick on Wayne and Paul
And they were sick on Miss.
Then everyone was shouting
All the children and Miss Phipps
Until Jason asked the driver,
'Can we stop for fish and chips?'

On our school trip to Scarborough
It wasn't that much fun,

Nothing really happened
And we never saw the sun.
We couldn't do a lot of things
Because of all the rain,
But if I have the chance next year
I'd love to go again!

Interrogation in the Nursery

Infant:	What's that?
INSPECTOR:	What?
Infant:	That on your face.
INSPECTOR:	It's a moustache.
Infant:	What does it do?
INSPECTOR:	It doesn't do anything.
Infant:	Oh.
INSPECTOR:	It just sits there on my lip.
Infant:	Does it go up your nose?
INSPECTOR:	No.
Infant:	Could I stroke it?
INSPECTOR:	No.
Infant:	Is it alive?
INSPECTOR:	No.
Infant:	Can I have one?
INSPECTOR:	No, little girls don't have moustaches.
Infant:	Why?
INSPECTOR:	Well, they just don't.
Infant:	Can I have one when I grow up?
INSPECTOR:	No, ladies don't have moustaches either.
Infant:	Well, my grannie's got one!

Christmas Lights

The lights on the Christmas tree winked,
And the snow fell thick and heavy outside.
From the walls of the school hall
Angels spread their silver wings
And the three kings held high their gifts.
The lights dimmed and silence fell.
Mums and dads, grannies and grampas,
Stared at the stage expectantly
For The Christmas Story to begin.

A spotlight flooded the stage and a small child entered.
Wide-eyed, she stared at the sea of smiling faces
before her.
'Welcome,' she whispered, 'to our ... to our ...'
Then, she froze like a frightened rabbit,
Caught in the headlight's glare.
'To our Nativity!' came the teacher's hushed
voice, off-stage.
'To our ...' began the child again. 'To our ...'
'Nativity!' repeated the teacher.
'Harvest Festival,' announced the child.

Too Clever by Half

I am so very good at everything,
I really am the best,
Brilliant at number work,
The top in every test,
My English book's outstanding,
And much better than the rest.
Oh, I really am a very clever girl.

I am extremely musical,
My voice is quite sublime.
I sing sweeter than the nightingale,
No voice compares to mine.
I play the cello beautifully,
I really sound divine.
Oh, I really am a very clever girl.

I'm particularly sporty,
And excel in every game:
Netball, hockey, badminton,
To me they're all the same,
And if the team I play with loses,
Well, I'm certainly not to blame.
Oh, I really am a very clever girl.

I am a very pretty child,
A little English rose.
With long blonde curls and
    large blue eyes,
And a little button nose.
My hands and face are always clean,
And so are all my clothes.
Oh, I really am a very clever girl.

I therefore find it rather strange
That no one plays with me.
Nobody ever telephones
Or asks me round for tea.
I don't have any friends at all.
Now, why ever should that be ?
Because I really am a very clever girl.

Holiday to Remember

The highlight of the holiday
(Well, it certainly was for me),
Was when we went to Waterworld
At Wilmington-on-Sea.

We swam and splashed in the salt-sea pool,
And went on every ride,
But the best part of the holiday
Was when Grandma blocked the slide.

The Cosmic Whirl at Waterworld,
Is really, really high,
It twists and turns like a slippery snake,
And reaches to the sky.

Well, Grandma thought she'd try it
And she clambered to the top,
Then she starting sliding really fast,
We thought she'd never stop!

But the Cosmic Whirl was narrow
And Grandma's pretty wide.
And soon she started slowing down,
And then – she blocked the slide.

She wriggled and she jiggled,
And she struggled to be free
But Gran was stuck in the Cosmic Whirl
At Wilmington-on-Sea.

The man who was behind her,
Like a bullet from a gun,
Set off down at such a speed
And crashed into my gran.

She flung herself around him,
The poor man was garrotted,
Then their arms and legs got tangled up
And their bodies, they were knotted.

There were screams and yelps and howls for help
As they tumbled down and down,
And soon a crowd of swimmers
Had gathered all around.

Then Grandad, who was watching,
Turned to speak to me and Mum.
'Just take at look at Gran,' he laughed.
'She's certainly having fun.'

The lifeguard blew his whistle
And shouted from the side.
'You two out the water now,
No messing down the slide!'

My Monstrous Bear

When I was small,
My father would pretend to be a monstrous bear.
He'd crawl about the floor on all fours
And his great ferocious eyes
Would stare and glare, searching for me.
He'd roar and roar
And growl and grunt,
And I would hide behind the chair,
And squeal and squirm
And feel the hair on my head stand up,
Excited in my fear.
He'd pretend not to see me
And lumber off and curl up on the rug
And snore and snore.
I would creep so quietly
And snuggle up, deep between his great warm paws.
My monstrous bear would hold me tightly
Keeping me from harm.

Reading Round the Class

On Friday we have reading round the class.
Kimberley Bloomer is the best.
She sails slowly along the page like a great galleon
And everyone looks up and listens.
'Beautiful reading, Kimberley, dear,' sighs Mrs Scott,
'And with such fluency, such feeling.
It's a delight to hear.'

On Friday we have reading round the class.
I'M THE WORST.
I stumble and mumble along slowly like a
broken-down train
And everyone looks up and listens.
Then, they smile and snigger and whisper behind
their hands.
'Dear me,' sighs Mrs Scott, 'rather rusty, Simon.
Quite a bit of practice needed, don't you think?
Too much television and football, that's your trouble,
And not enough reading.'

AND SHE WONDERS WHY I DON'T LIKE BOOKS.

41

Conversation at the School Gates

You, boy!

What?

When you talk to a teacher you say, 'Sir.'

What … Sir?

What are you doing?

Nothing … Sir.

Exactly. Nothing!

What?

Sir! You say, 'Sir.'

What … Sir?

You are doing nothing!

That's what I just said … Sir.

Well, why are you just sitting on the wall when everyone else is in school working?

I'm having a rest … Sir.

Oh, you're having a rest, are you?

That's right … Sir.

What's your name?

Darren.

Darren what?

Sir.

No, no, what's your second name?

Wayne.

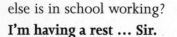

42

Your last name!

Porter ... Sir.

Now look here, Porter, I don't like your attitude at all. The bell has gone, everyone's in school and you're sitting idly on the school wall doing nothing. Furthermore, you are not in uniform.

That's right ... Sir.

Well, get into school and I will see you in my room for detention at the end of the day.

I can't ... Sir.

Give me one good reason why you can't, Porter.

I work over the road. I left this school last year ... Sir.

The Way I Am

I'm just an ordinary sort of boy,
Not the centre of attention,
The best of the bunch,
Apple of the teacher's eye,
The one everyone remembers.
IT'S JUST THE WAY I AM.

I'm just an ordinary sort of boy,
Not the high flier,
Captain of the team,
Star of the school play,
Top of the class.
IT'S JUST THE WAY I AM.

I'm just an ordinary sort of boy,
Nothing special at all,
Run of the mill,
Fair to middling,
No great shakes.
IT'S JUST THE WAY I AM.

I'm just an ordinary sort of boy,
But I'm not invisible.
I do exist!
I'm as different as anyone else,
There's nobody like me.
And to my family, I'm pretty special.
So please, Sir, please, Miss – notice **ME** sometimes.
I AM WHAT I AM.

Samantha-Jayne

Nobody speaks to Samantha-Jayne,
The silent child with the fancy name,
Who comes to school with hair a mess,
And milk stains down her dirty dress,
Who wears a coat that's far too small,
And stands alone by the playground wall.

Nobody plays with Samantha-Jayne,
Who lives with her mum down Leadmill Lane,
In a run-down flat that's dark and smelly,
Who spends her nights glued to the telly,
And sleeps in a bed that's damp and cold,
In a dark little room that's full of mould.

Nobody cares about Samantha-Jayne,
Who walks to school in wind and rain,
With her unwashed face and hair a mess,
And her coat too small and her dirty dress,
With the tight little mouth and the frightened stare.
No one, no one is there to care.

Samantha-Jayne, Samantha-Jayne
Oh, what do you dream of, Samantha-Jayne,
As you walk to school all alone
Or stand in the playground on your own?

Do you dream of friends with whom to play,
To help you through the lonely day?
Do you dream of arms to hold you tight
To help you through the lonely night?

Leaving Home

When Matthew was seven,
He decided to leave home.
He packed his little bag
And tucked his teddy underneath his arm,
And said, 'I'm going. I've had enough.'
'Why are you leaving, Matty?' asked Dad.
'Because you shouted at me.'
'No I didn't. I never raised my voice.'
'You shouted at me with your eyes,' said Matthew.
'Shall I run you to the station?' asked Dad.
'No, I'll get a bus.'
'Well, goodbye then, Matty,' said Dad, opening the door
On to the cold, black night beyond.
Matthew peered into the darkness.
'And be careful of the wolves,' said Dad.
'I'm not going now,' replied Matthew.
'I've changed my mind.'

The School Inspector Calls

Miss, Miss, there's a man at the back of the classroom,
With a big black book and a smile like a crocodile.
Miss, he asked me if I've got a lot of homework,
And when I said, 'Too much!' – he wrote it down.

Miss, Miss, there's a man at the back of the classroom,
With a long, sharp pencil and eyes like a basking shark.
Miss, he asked me what I liked best about our school
And when I said, 'The dinners!' – he wrote it down.

Miss, Miss, there's a man at the back of the classroom
With a big square badge and hair like a hedgehog.
Miss, I asked him what he liked best about our school
And he said he was not there to answer my questions,
He said he was just 'a fly on the wall'.

Miss, Miss, why don't you tell him to 'BUZZ OFF!'

Earwax

'It's wax,' explained the doctor,
Shining a little torch into Dominic's ear.
'Your son's got wax in his ear.'
'Earwax,' Dad said relieved.
'His brothers both had wax in their ears when they were
    his age.
It must run in the family.
It's nature's way of protecting the ear from water.
That's what we were told by the nurse.'
'That's very true,' said the doctor, peering into the ear.
'Yes, my other sons had wax in their ears too,' said Dad.
    And had to have them syringed.
I suppose it will be the same for Dominic?'
'No, no,' replied the doctor, inserting a pair of silver
    tweezers
And extracting something round and red and shaped
    like a bullet.
'Not for a wax crayon.'

Auntie Penny's Pets

Auntie Penny has a parrot,
She calls him Captain Jack.
He has red and yellow feathers
And a beak of shiny black.
He has eyes like tiny pebbles,
And claws of scaly grey,
And he squawks and talks,
And talks and squawks,
All the livelong day.

Auntie Penny has a Scotty dog,
She calls him Mr Mac.
He has little legs and a stumpy tail,
And a very hairy back.
He has teeth as sharp as icicles,
And eyes like diamonds bright,
And he snaps and yaps,
And yaps and snaps,
Morning, noon and night.

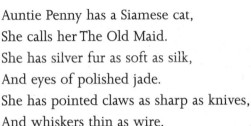

Auntie Penny has a Siamese cat,
She calls her The Old Maid.
She has silver fur as soft as silk,
And eyes of polished jade.
She has pointed claws as sharp as knives,
And whiskers thin as wire,

And she purrs and purrs,
And never stirs,
Curled up by the fire.

Auntie Penny has a donkey,
She calls him Irish Brian.
He is small and thin and bony,
With hooves as hard as iron.
He has teeth as square as tombstones,
And a mane as red as rust,
And he neighs and brays,
And brays and neighs,
From daylight until dusk.

Auntie Penny has a portly pig,
She calls her Mrs Stout.
She is round and fat and bristly,
With a wet and wiggly snout.
She has a curly tail like a coiled-up spring,
And a coat of purest white,
And she grunts and digs,
With the other pigs,
From daybreak until night.

Auntie Penny has a husband,
His name is Uncle Paul.
He's very, very quiet,
In fact, he hardly speaks at all.

He cooks and cleans and washes,
And tidies all the house,
And he tiptoes round,
Without a sound,
As quiet as a mouse.

Auntie Penny, she likes all her pets:
The Old Maid and Captain Jack,
Mrs Stout and Irish Brian,
And grumpy Mr Mac,
But she has a special favourite,
He's the quietest of them all,
And she loves him best,
More than all the rest,
And his name is Uncle Paul.

Bee in the Classroom

One Friday, in through the open window of the classroom
Flew the biggest bee in the whole, wide world –
A big, round, black and yellow, bumbling monster.
It buzzed and buzzed,
And hummed and hummed,
And bobbed and bobbed,
Above everybody's head.

'Miss! Miss!' screamed Bernadette,
'There's a bee in the classroom!'
'Just ignore it,' said the teacher,
'And get on with your writing.
If you don't bother the bee, Bernadette,
The bee won't bother you.'

'Miss! Miss!' yelled Barry,
'Shall I swot it with my ruler?'
'Certainly not,' said the teacher,
'It has as much a right to life as any living creature.
If you don't bother the bee, Barry,
The bee won't bother you.'

'Miss! Miss!' suggested Betty,
'Shall I catch it in my pencil case?'

'Not a very good idea,' said the teacher,
'That would make it very angry.
If you don't bother the bee, Betty,
The bee won't bother you.'

One Friday, in through the open window of the classroom
Flew the biggest bee in the whole, wide world –
A big, round, black and yellow, bumbling monster.
It buzzed and buzzed around the teacher's desk,
It hummed and hummed about her ear,
It bobbed and bobbed before her eyes,
And then it stung her on the nose.

Teachers, you know, can sometimes be wrong!

Remembrance Day

On Remembrance Sunday Grandpa cried
For his two brothers, who had died
In some forgotten, far-off land,
Of blistering heat and burning sand.
He touched a medal on his chest
Which sparkled brighter than the rest.
'The Africa Star,' he gently sighed,
'A badge of honour and worn with pride,
A symbol of our Ted and Jack,
Who never made the journey back.'
We watched old soldiers stride on by,
Straight of back and heads held high,
And clutched our poppies of brightest red,
And cried for the brothers, Jack and Ted.

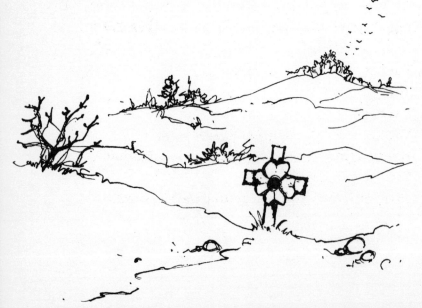

The Last Word

My big brother likes to have the last word.
Yesterday Dad said to him, 'I wish you wouldn't always argue with me.'
'I don't,' said Dominic.
'You do,' said Dad.
'I don't.'
'There you go again.'
'What?'
'Arguing with me.'
'I'm not arguing.'
'You are.'
'I'm not.'
'You see what I mean?'
'No.'
'Of course you do.'
'I don't know what you mean.'
'Arguing with me.'
'I'm not arguing,' said Dominic.
'You are,' said Dad.
'I'm not.'
'Well, what are you doing now then?'
'Having a difference of opinion,' replied Dominic.
'That's arguing,' said Dad.
'No it isn't,' said Dominic, getting the last word.

Please Leave on the Light!

Oh, leave the landing light on, Mum,
Oh, please leave on the light.
Oh, leave the landing light on, Mum,
I can't make it through the night.

I'm frightened in my room alone,
When the moon is shining bright,
And shadows dance across the walls,
Oh, please leave on the light.

I have these awful, scary thoughts
Of creatures in the night,
With long curved claws and massive jaws,
Oh, please leave on the light.

I hear them underneath the bed,
Scuttling out of sight,
Waiting for the darkness.
Oh, please leave on the light.

Then, they slither out so silently,
And give me such a fright,
With their cold, cold breath and icy hands,
Oh, please leave on the light.

They clamber on the eiderdown,
With golden eyes so bright,
And clasp me in their monstrous arms.
Oh, please leave on the light.

I fear their breath upon my cheek,
I dread their teeth that bite.
I cannot bear the thought of them,
Oh, please leave on the light.

Oh, Mummy, Mummy, do not leave,
Oh, Mummy hold me tight.
I know that I'll have nightmares,
If you don't leave on the light.

Come, come, my dear, his mother said,
I think it only right,
You're forty-seven years old, you know,
So, I'm turning off the light!

The Pirate

When I was six my father told me
Great Uncle Alex, who I had never met,
Was coming for a visit.
'He's very old,' my father said, 'and rather stern.
He has no children of his own, you see,
So, on your best behaviour, please.
He was a pirate,' said my father casually,
'And has travelled round the world.'

When I heard the doorbell ring,
I scurried to my room, too scared to meet him.
I could not face the figure with the cutlass in his hand,
And the great curved pistols poking from his belt.
I dared not stare into that cruel and rugged face,
And look upon the great hooked nose and tangled hair,
And see the ear with dangling ring of gold,
And meet the black patch covering an eye.

I cried and cried when Father came to fetch me.
He was red-faced and far from pleased
To find me curled up, whimpering on my bed.
'I said your best behaviour!' Father snapped,
And took me down to meet the buccaneer himself.
To my surprise he was an old, old man,
With gentle eyes and wrinkled, friendly face,
A tiny figure, frail, in shiny suit and polished shoes.

'This is your Uncle Alex,' Father said.
'He did what many boys would like to do
When they've grown up: to fly a plane
And travel round the world – and be a pilot.'

Top Twenty Things That Parents Never Say

- Of course you can have more pocket money.
- I bought those chocolate biscuits just for you.
- No, it won't hurt to leave your bike out in the rain.
- The telephone is free if you wish to use it.
- Don't bother with the dishes, I'll do them later.
- I do wish the school wouldn't give you so much homework.
- I like your friend with the nose stud and the tattoos.
- You're not coming in too early tonight, are you?
- Just leave your dirty underwear on the floor.
- Don't worry, I came bottom of the class when I was your age.
- I hope you enjoy the rest of the late-night film.
- Would you like any help sticking that poster on your bedroom wall?
- These trainers are very cheap.
- Would you like lots of greasy food at your all-night party?
- I don't think the dog's ready for a walk yet.
- Why don't you stay in bed a little longer this morning?
- I do hate a tidy room.
- Leave all the lights on, will you?
- Don't bother cleaning out the bath.
- School holidays are a bit short this year.

Lizzie's Road

Little Lizzie drew a long, long road
That curled across the paper like a strange, exotic snake.
She decorated it in darkest reds and brightest blues,
Gleaming golds and glittering greens.
Mum asked, 'Why all these wonderful colours?'
'These are the rubies and emeralds and pearls,'
     Lizzie explained.
'The diamonds and opals and precious stones.'
'What a wonderful road,' said Mum. 'Is it magic?'
'No,' explained the child. 'It's just a jewel carriageway.'

When I Am Old

'My grannie wobbles, you know,' said the child.
'She's very old, you see, and has an illness.
It makes her tremble so and shake her head
And sometimes say things we don't understand.
We wheel her round the garden in her chair,
And help her with her tea and wipe her mouth,
And sometimes comb her soft and silvery hair.
It has a special name, my Grannie's illness.
"Old Timers' Disease" the doctor calls it.'

If, when I'm old and trembling and I shake my head,
And someone helps me with my tea,
And wipes my mouth and combs my silvery hair,
Please let her say I have 'Old Timers' Disease'.
It's rather warm and comforting, I think.

The Day Mum Brought the Baby Home

When Mum brought the baby home,
Everyone forgot about me.
Grannie cooed, 'Ooooooooooo, isn't she beoooooootiful?'
Grandpa cried, 'Ehhhhhhhhhhhh, isn't she luvvvvvvvely?'
Auntie Christine sighed, 'Ohhhhhhhhhhhh, isn't she
    gorrrrrrrrrgeous?'
Uncle Michael chortled, 'Aaahhhhhh, isn't she
    amaaaaaaazing?'
Even the brothers said, 'Wow, isn't she cool?'
Then they looked in my direction.
I said to them all, 'Are you all asking me?
Because, if you are, I don't agree.

'She has no teeth, is bald and fat,
I'd sooner have a dog or cat.
Well, they don't dribble down your clothes,
Poke your eyes and squeeze your nose,
Slaver, gurgle, drool and slurp,
Slobber, bubble, spit and burp,
Wet tons of nappies all the time,
And scream and moan and mewl and whine.'

Everyone looked shocked.

'I thought you'd love your little baby sister,' said Dad sadly.

'I do love her,' I replied smiling.

'I'm just trying to get a bit of attention around here,
That's all!'

Let's Face It

Have you heard about:
The conductor who faced the music,
The statistician who faced the facts,
The twins who came face to face,
The accountant who knew the face value,
The pilot who flew in the face of,
The sunbather who went red in the face,
The soldier who put a brave face on it,
The lifeguard who saved face,
The gambler who had a poker face,
The actor who showed his face,
The violinist who had a face as long as a fiddle,
The miner who was face down,
The acrobat who fell flat on his face,
The weightlifter who had a face lift,
The chef who had egg on his face,
The cleaner who wiped the smile off his face and
The naturist who had a bare-faced cheek?

Remember Me?

'Do you remember me?' asked the young man.
The old man at the bus stop,
Shabby, standing in the sun, alone,
Looked round.
He stared for a moment, screwing up his eyes,
Then shook his head.
'No, I don't remember you.'
'You used to teach me,' said the young man.
'I've taught so many,' said the old man, sighing,
'I forget.'
'I was the boy you said was useless,
Good for nothing, a waste of space.
Who always left your classroom crying,
And dreaded every lesson that you taught.'
The old man shook his head and turned away.
'No, I don't remember you,' he murmured.
'Well, I remember you,' the young man said.

If You Go Down to the Woods Today

If you go down to the woods today,
You're sure of a big surprise.
We're chopping down the trees, you see,
Before your very eyes.
The pines and ash and poplars,
They all are coming down,
To make a smart new ring road,
To circle round the town.
The cedar, cherry, chestnut,
The beech and elm and briar,
We're going to pile them all up high,
And set them all afire.
The willow, maple, alder,
The silver birch and oak,
We're going to make a great big blaze,
And they'll go up in smoke.
The sycamore and mountain ash,
Yes, every one must go
To be replaced by motorway,
That's progress, don't you know.
So if you've nothing else to do,
Well, why not grab a saw,
And help us build a bonfire.
Isn't that what trees are for?

Five Clerihews

Elizabeth said, 'I'm like a queen,
In my new dress of vivid green.'
Her brother Matt let out a scream,
'You're a wee bit early for Halloween!'

Our neighbour talking to my mum said,
'So I gave her a piece of my mind.'
To part with such a precious thing,
She must be very kind.

Mr Wilson wears a wig,
But for his head it's rather big.
In windy weather he was careless,
Now Mr Wilson's head is hairless.

'Do you want a smacked bottom, my lad?'
Asked my father in threatening voice.
I'm not likely to say, 'Yes, please, Father dear,'
I don't think I've much of a choice!

I wrote a note to Auntie Netta,
'I hope you get this little letter.
Thank you for the woolly sweater,
But on the sheep it would look much better.'

Today, I Feel

Today, I feel as:

Pleased as PUNCH,
Fit as a FIDDLE,
Keen as a KNIFE,
Hot as a GRIDDLE,
Bold as BRASS,
Bouncy as a BALL,
Keen as MUSTARD,
High as a WALL,
Bright as a BUTTON,
Light as a FEATHER,
Fresh as a DAISY,
Fragrant as HEATHER,
Chirpy as a CRICKET,
Sound as a BELL,
Sharp as a NEEDLE,
Deep as a WELL,
High as a KITE,
Strong as a BULL,
Bubbly as BATH WATER,
Warm as WOOL,
Clean as a new PIN,
Shiny as MONEY,
Quick as LIGHTNING,
Sweet as HONEY,

Cool as a CUCUMBER,
Fast as a HARE,
Right as RAIN,
Brave as a BEAR,
Lively as a MONKEY,
Busy as a BEE,
Good as GOLD,
Free as the SEA.

I'M SO HAPPY – I'M JUST LOST FOR WORDS.

Supply Teacher

The supply teacher wears a wig.
He doesn't think anyone knows – but we do.
It's like a ginger tomcat sitting on his head,
A shaggy red rug, a furry mat, a coloured thatch of hair.
Once, when he sneezed it slid slightly forward
And he didn't notice – but we did.
When he saw us smiling and smirking he asked angrily,
'What's so funny?'
We started to giggle and wriggle in our seats
Biting our fists and covering our mouths
To stop ourselves from laughing.
'What's so funny?' he roared. 'What's so funny?'
'Keep your hair on,' came a whisper from the back.

Interview with the Headmaster

You wanted to see me, headmaster?

Yes, come in, Poskitt, and close the door.

Yes, headmaster.

You are late again!

Yes, headmaster.

What's the excuse this time, Poskitt?

I'm afraid I overslept, headmaster.

Buy an alarm clock!

Yes, headmaster.

Where is your tie, Poskitt?

I forgot to put it on, headmaster.

You know the school rule about wearing a tie, don't you, Poskitt?

Yes, headmaster.

Are you wearing boots?

Yes, headmaster.

You know the rules about boots as well, don't you, Poskitt?

Yes, headmaster.

Well, don't wear them then!

No, headmaster.

And wear a tie!

Yes, headmaster.

And look at the state of your hair, Poskitt.

What about my hair, headmaster?

You haven't got any!

That's right, headmaster, it's the latest style.

What is?

My hair, headmaster.

But you haven't got any, Poskitt!

It's all the craze, headmaster.

Being bald?

Yes, headmaster.

And is that a tattoo, Poskitt?

Yes, headmaster. It's an eagle.

I can see what it is, Poskitt, and I don't like it.

I thought you were very fond of birds, headmaster?

I like them flying in the sky, Poskitt, not emblazoned on people's arms.

Yes, headmaster.

And what about the nose stud and the earrings?

What about the nose stud and the earrings, headmaster?

I don't like those either.

I thought they would make me look more interesting, headmaster.

You thought wrong, Poskitt.

Yes, headmaster.

You're letting the school down, Poskitt. You're giving a very poor impression.

Yes, headmaster.

I want to see a change in your attitude, Poskitt.

Yes, headmaster.

Otherwise you're out.

Yes, headmaster.

Pull your socks up, Poskitt, make an effort, set a better example.

Yes, headmaster.

And don't be late again.

No, headmaster.

And I'll see you at the staff meeting tonight, Poskitt.

Yes, headmaster.

First Love

Kimberley Bloomer wore sensible shoes
And a bright pink cardigan and snow-white socks.
Her hair was gathered in bunches and tied with red ribbons.
When she stared at me with those big blue eyes
I went all wobbly at the knees.

Kimberley Bloomer was the best reader in the class.
Her voice was as soft as a summer night
And her smile made me tremble.
I sat next to her for two days,
And she smelt of flowers and lavender soap.

Kimberley Bloomer helped me with my writing.
I remember her long fingers
With nails like little pink seashells.
When I got things wrong she sighed,
And I felt all funny deep inside.

Kimberley Bloomer moved away.
I never saw her again.
All year I ached for Kimberley Bloomer.

Dad's Diet

My dad's gone on a diet.
It happens every year.
He starts just after Christmas,
When he gives up crisps and beer.
He stares into the mirror,
And he holds his stomach in,
'My goodness me,' he says to Mum,
'I've got a double chin!'
It's then that we stop talking,
And the house goes deathly quiet.
'Yes,' sighs Dad, 'I'm getting fat.
I'm going on a diet.
I shall have to give up chocolate cake,
Fried potatoes, sirloin steak,
Mushroom omelettes, savoury dips,
Egg and bacon, fish and chips,
Butter, biscuits, raspberry jam,
Fillet of pork and leg of lamb,
Sausages, burgers, Sunday roast,
Pasta, trifle, cheese on toast,
Sticky buns and ice cream cones,
Pasties, pastries, tarts and scones,
The only food upon my plate
Is that which helps me lose some weight.
Bowls of fruit and lots of greens

Carrots, cabbage, sprouts and beans,
Apples, oranges, pears and lemons
Peaches, prunes, plums and melons
Natural yoghurt, wholemeal wheat,
Organic bran and fat-free meat,
Slimmers soup, low-calorie spread,
Orange juice and butterless bread
Plums, tomatoes, tangerines,
Low cholesterol margarines.'
Yes, my dad goes on this diet,
But his willpower's pretty weak.
He starts just after Christmas,
And it lasts about a week.

Unlucky Uncle Eric

Unlucky Uncle Eric
While one day playing cricket,
Saw a four-leaf clover
And thought that he would pick it.
As he bent down towards the ground,
To pluck the lucky leaf,
The cricket ball flew through the air
And knocked out all his teeth.
He shouted, 'Drat!' and dropped the bat,
Which landed on his toes,
It bounced back up and cracked his chin,
Then smacked him on the nose.
Smeared in blood and caked in mud,
He said, 'I'm glad that's over,'
Then with a sigh, he held up high,
His lucky four-leaf clover.

Bilingualist

My father speaks two languages,
Should you hear him, you'd agree.
He has a language for the baby,
And a language just for me.

Now when he's speaking just to me,
I understand each word,
But when he's with the baby,
He really sounds absurd.

It goes something like this:

Who's Daddy's little poppet?
Who's Mummy's sugar plum?
Who's Grannie's diddy dumpling?
Whose Grampa's honey bun?

Ah, see those ickle fingers,
Ah, see that nibbly nose,
Ah, see those pwitty peepers,
Ah, see those ickle toes.

Doody, doody, doody,
Diddums, diddums, do,
Flopsy, wopsy, wopsy,
Itchy, kitchy coo.

Now if I had the courage,
(But sadly I have not),
I'd say, 'I'll hold the baby, Dad,
And you get in the cot!'

Secret Love

'Oh tell me, tell me, Lizzie, please
Just what did Jason say.
I know he told you not to tell
But tell me anyway.
When he looks across the room
I go weak at the knees.
Do you think he's going to ask me out?
Oh tell me, Lizzie, please.
Did he say he liked me best?
Or does he like Louise?
Or is it Sue or Jane or Pam?
Oh tell me, Lizzie, please.
I've got to know what Jason said,
Oh, Liz, don't be a tease.
I promise I won't say a word
Oh tell me, Lizzie, please.'
'Well, can you keep a secret?'
Asked Lizzie, with a sigh.
'Of course I can,' her friend replied,
And Liz said, 'So can I!'

Night Noises

Our house is full of noises,
I hear them every night.
They start as soon as I'm in bed
And have just turned off the light.

Tap drips,
Toilet flushes,
Sink gurgles,
Shower gushes,
Door bangs,
Stair creaks,
Chair scrapes,
Cupboard squeaks,
Doorbell buzzes,
Dishes rattle,
Washer hums,
Fire crackles,
Curtain rustles,
Lock clicks,
Telephone rings,
Clock ticks.

But soon the house goes very quiet.
It gets to be quite boring –
Until my dad climbs into bed
And starts his nightly snoring.

He grunts and growls and yawns and groans,
Mumbles, murmurs, sighs and moans,
Huffs and puffs and pants and mutters,
Yawns and whimpers, huffs and splutters.

His snoring makes the floorboards quake,
The wardrobe rattle, the windows shake,
The timbers groan, the bed vibrate.
I put the pillow over my head,
And snuggle down deep inside the bed,
But the noise Dad makes would wake the dead.

He grunts and growls and yawns and groans,
Mumbles, murmurs, sighs and moans,
Huffs and puffs and pants and mutters,
Yawns and whimpers, huffs and splutters.

Then, in the morning down he'll creep
And ask, 'Did everyone have a good night's sleep?'

Losing Your Marbles

The bags were packed,
The lights turned off,
The milk cancelled,
The garage locked,
The gates closed
And we were all set for our holiday.

And then ... Dominic said ... 'I've swallowed a marble!'
'What!' shrieked Mum.
'What!' roared Dad.
'What!' laughed the brothers.
'What!' giggled Lizzie.
'I've swallowed a marble!' howled Dominic.

'How did you manage to do that?' asked Dad.
'I just popped it in my mouth and swallowed it,'
moaned Dominic.
'What made you put it in your mouth?' asked Mum.
'I was pretending it was a sweet,' groaned Dominic.
'It might never come out,' said Lizzie, nodding.
'They'll have to cut him open,' agreed the brothers.

At the hospital Mum told the doctor,
'He's swallowed a marble.'
The doctor smiled like a hungry vampire

And put his ear to Dominic's tummy.
'I can hear it rolling about inside,' he said.
'Please don't cut me open!' cried Dominic.

The doctor gave Mum some medicine.
It was thick and pink and in a large brown bottle.
'Three times a day,' he said. 'That should do the trick.
What went in one way should come out the other.'
Next day in the bathroom we heard a clunk and a cry,
'I've got my marble back!' yelled Dominic.

Index of First Lines